James Rae

BLUE
SAXOPHONE DUETS

UE 14051
ISMN 979-0-008-04920-0
UPC 8-03452-03521-3
ISBN 978-3-7024-4354-2

PREFACE

This collection of pieces has been composed with the aim of introducing saxophonists to duets in the blues idiom. The pieces are of moderate length and in varied styles.

Chord symbols have been included at concert pitch to accompany both E♭ and B♭ instruments. There is also a separate Part 2 for B♭ Tenor Saxophone if Part 1 is to be played by E♭ Alto Saxophone.

VORWORT

Die vorliegende Sammlung soll Saxophonisten die Möglichkeit geben, sich mit dem Duospiel im Bluesstil vertraut zu machen. Die Stücke sind von maßiger Länge und decken eine ganze Reihe von Stilrichtungen ab.

Die Stimmen enthalten Akkordsymbole in Konzerthöhe zur Begleitung von Es- und B-Saxophonen. Darüberhinaus umfaßt der Band auch eine eigene 2 Stimme für Tenorsaxophon in B, falls die 1 Stimme mit Altsaxophon in Es gespielt werden soll.

CONTENTS

Chinese Whispers	2
Tuff Stuff!	4
Back Street Blues	6
Junction Five	8
Recorded Delivery	10

Chinese Whispers

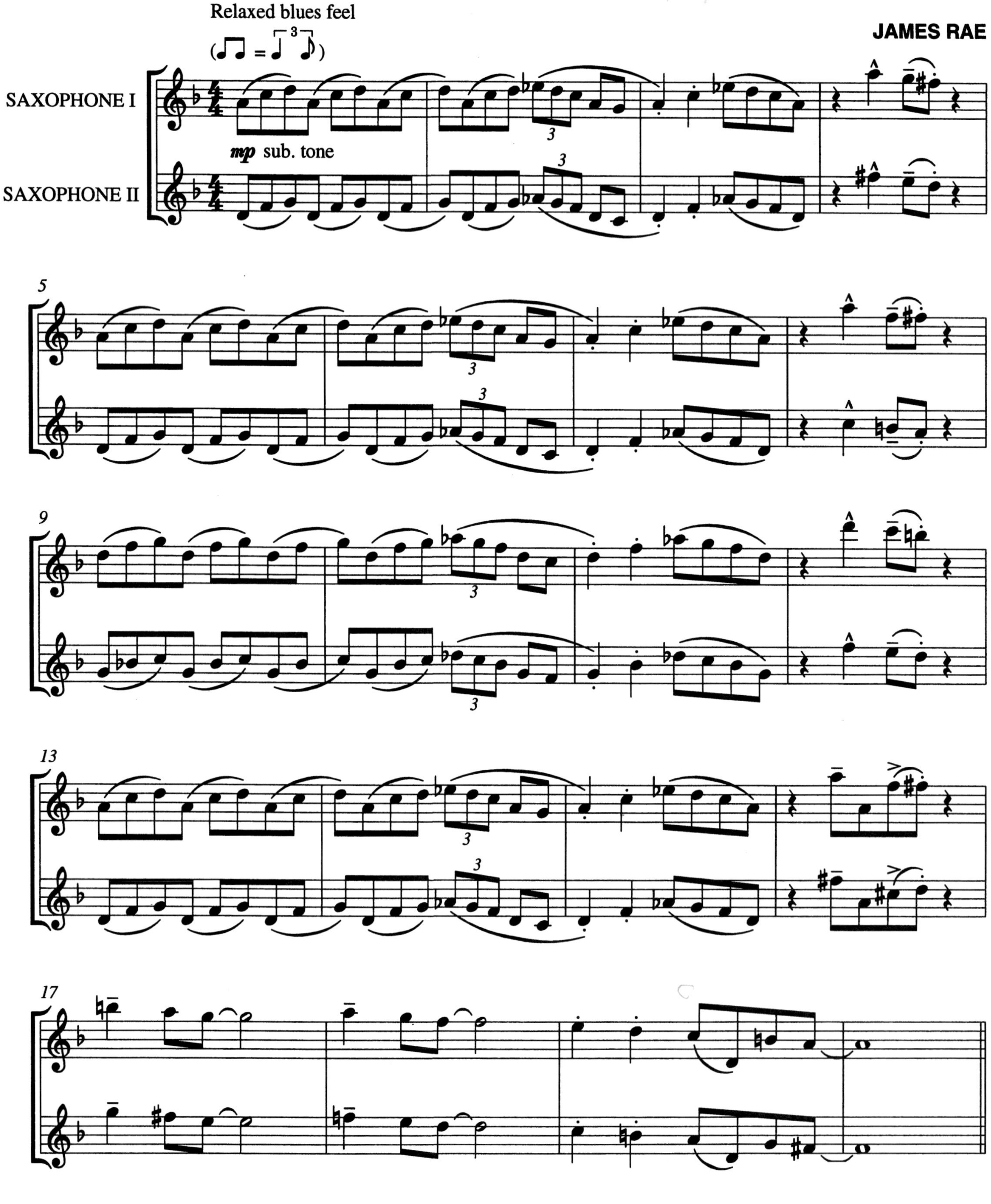

JAMES RAE

Tuff Stuff!

Back Street Blues

JAMES RAE

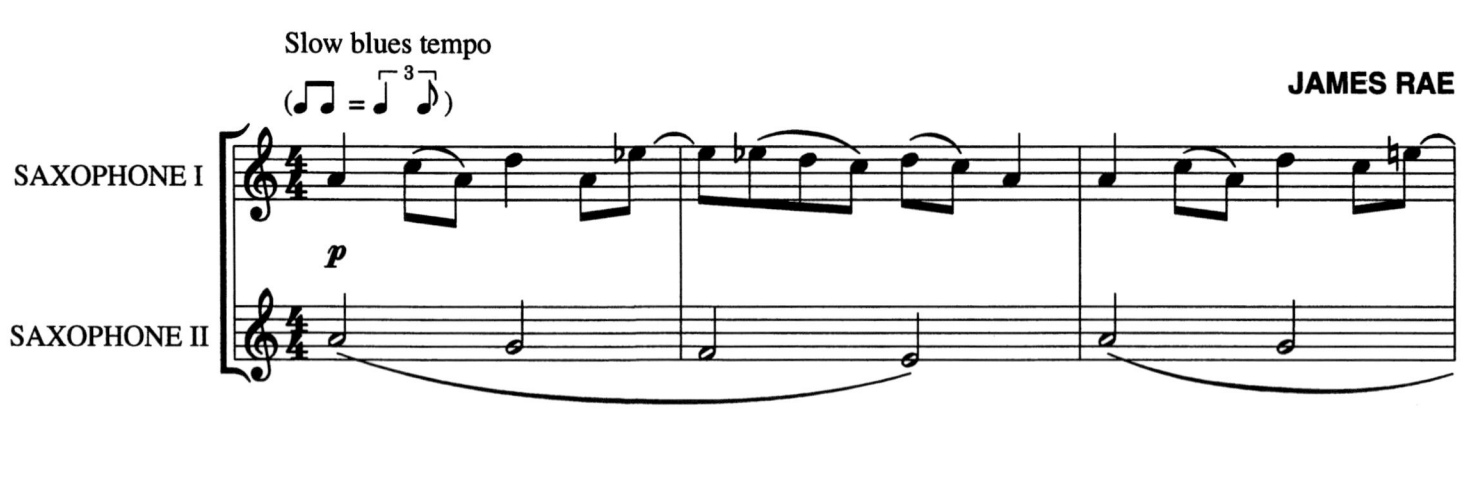

UE 14051

Junction Five

JAMES RAE

Recorded Delivery

JAMES RAE